"*No Sugar-Coating: The Coffee* ... curate, and poignant capture ... ities involved. Jillana's book is wonderful preparation for anyone considering becoming a foster parent and important validation for those already doing this critical work."

— MIRIAM GREEN, MA, LPC
Senior Operations Manager (retired)
Department of Human Services Child Welfare

"Jillana's *No Sugar-Coating* letter is something I wish I could have every prospective foster parent read! Even experienced foster parents can find in this letter the comfort of not being alone on a journey with both difficult and wonderful experiences. Jillana is able to capture the realities of foster parenting and presents it in a genuine and heartfelt way. There are many experiences people may wonder about but are afraid to ask, and this letter gently covers all of these topics with grace and a sense of humor. Thank you, Jillana, for sharing your personal experiences and supporting so many families who are considering sharing their home with children who need stability, comfort, and time to heal."

— ANANI KUFFNER, MSW, CSWA
Caseworker and Trainer
Department of Human Services Child Welfare

"Jillana Goble's letter to prospective caregivers is honest, compassionate, and real. She tells both the beautiful and terrible stories that comprise caregiving in a down to earth and readable manner. Anyone considering fostering or adopting should sit down and read this book before taking the next step."

— FRANNIE MCMAHON
Foster Care and Adoption Training Specialist
Portland State University Child Welfare Partnership

"Jillana has drawn upon her years of personal experiences and put together a book that speaks honestly to the often-hard reality of what fostering can look like, while weaving in the immutable hope that is so easy to lose sight of. I highly recommend this book to anyone who is considering fostering, anyone who is in the midst of fostering, and even to those who want to support someone dear to them who is fostering."

— NICK
Foster Parent

"Seven years ago, as a prospective foster parent, I had the privilege of hearing from Jillana and her husband, Luke, with a hot cup of coffee in hand. Her story then was as helpful as it is now. This letter is a must-read for anyone considering becoming a foster parent. Jillana offers honest yet hopeful insight into the journey ahead and peels back the many layers of being a healthy parent to vulnerable kids. She shares tremendous insight into the day-to-day considerations for navigating your fostering journey while also highlighting the mental and emotional side of being sustained for the long haul."

— SARA
Foster Parent

"Jillana's nuggets on foster care are birthed out of realistic hope and hard-earned experience walking the walk of all she's talking about in this book. If you're considering stepping into the life of foster parenting, her voice is one worth listening to as you jump into the beautiful and complex unknown. As someone who's fostering because of her encouragement and wisdom, I know I couldn't do it without the stories, wisdom, and love included here."

— SETH
Foster Parent

"Jillana's book is a must read for anyone entertaining foster care—young, old, married, single, with kids or without! She gives a no holds barred account of hers and many others' experiences when it comes to parenting vulnerable children and engaging all that comes with them. Her realistic, yet optimistic, approach to life in foster care is a breath of fresh air and is the real deal! I wish I would have had something like this to read while I was toying with the idea of becoming a foster parent—it is a wealth of knowledge and encouragement!"

— EMILY
Foster Parent

"In *No Sugar-Coating*, Jillana shares many of the same nuggets that she has shared with me in person over the last five years I have been a foster parent. Jillana is straightforward about her experiences and learned wisdom. This is a must read for anyone who has ever considered becoming a foster parent to learn about the realities of the journey ahead."

— KAT
Foster Parent

No Sugar-Coating

Also by Jillana Goble

A Love-Stretched Life:
Stories on Wrangling Hope, Embracing the Unexpected,
and Discovering the Meaning of Family

No Sugar-Coating

THE COFFEE TALK YOU NEED ABOUT FOSTER PARENTING

JILLANA GOBLE

www.jillana-goble.com

Cover & interior design by Typewriter Creative Co.
Cover photos by Valerio Rosati & Avelina Studio on Creativemarket.com.

ISBN 978-1-7340584-0-6 (Paperback)
ISBN 978-1-7340584-1-3 (eBook)
ISBN 978-1-7340584-2-0 (Audiobook)

For those full of wide-eyed wonder, questions, and various emotions when considering becoming a foster parent, this book is for you.

For those already engaging the day-to-day of this road less traveled parenting reality, this book is for you as well.

Table of Contents

Introduction

"Hey, I hear you're a foster parent. I'd like to do that one day," she says eagerly, almost whimsically. She looks about twenty-six, the same age I was when I became a foster parent. She says this while filling her coffee cup at the back table at church, about to head into service after the first song has already started to play. As she splashes in the cream and swings her purse over her shoulder, she asks, *"Has it been hard?"* Her eyes are bright and earnest.

I smile. "Yes," I say.

"But has it been worth it?" she asks, flipping her long brown hair over her shoulder and already taking steps away from the coffee table and into the sanctuary.

There's just too much to say to respond with any kind of accuracy. So I settle for "It's hard *and* it's worth it," trying to sound hopeful without implying that it's a breeze. She mouths a voiceless "Thank you" as she slips into the service.

In my former life as a community college English as a Second Language instructor, small talk was always one of the hardest aspects of teaching immigrants and refugees about American culture. It was challenging as we role-played in advanced ESL classes that "How are you?" and "How's it going?" are often just another form of saying "Hello." Many people who ask the question are not prepared to stop, engage, and actually hear the answer.

The same can apply to questions on-the-fly about foster care.

In an ideal world, a coffee date would be the next best place to start, but drinking a pot of coffee and taking up space at a cozy table in the corner still wouldn't be enough to convey how much my foster care journey has transformed me as a person.

I humbly write this letter, explaining the things I wish someone had shared with me when I began my fostering journey in 2003. Should you choose to foster, I want you to be as prepared as possible.

Additionally, I founded a grass-roots movement, Embrace Oregon, which has been the catalyst for the state-wide initiative, Every Child. I continue to have the privilege of interacting with countless prospective and current foster parents, as well as those who work with our state's Child Welfare agency in many roles.

For your reading ease, I broke this letter up into seven primary sections. Please know these aren't perfect delineations as many areas ebb and flow into one another.

As we prepare to dive in, I want to share three things:

1) I literally didn't know a single person who had ever been a foster parent before becoming one. I only knew the hazy concept of foster care. Now, after more than a decade-and-a-half of personal experience, as well as walking alongside others, I desire to share with you some educational, practical, emotional, and hard-fought snippets of wisdom I have learned (sometimes the hard way) about foster-parenting.

2) I have direct experience with the two primary ways people be-come foster parents. I have raised my hand to choose to willing-ly become a foster parent. Years later, I was also tapped on the shoulder by a state agency asking me to be a foster parent for a specific child related to me. Both journeys are unique and chal-lenging. While I do not focus on the specific challenges of being a relative foster parent, this letter has relatable truths to people fostering in both categories.

3) More than anything, I wish someone had sat me down, looked me in the eye, and told me this non-sugar-coated-truth: Foster care is a constant invitation to walk a precarious tightrope be-tween reality and hope.

Dear Prospective Foster Parent,

You'll take 24 hours of training, but this will never fully prepare you. It's not necessarily because the training doesn't have appropriate materials or the facilitator isn't skilled, but because until you are *living* it, my friend, there's a certain amount of telling that will fall short.

My motivation for this letter is not to twist your arm and convince you that fostering is yours to do in this world; nor am I trying to talk you out of it. If you choose to proceed with becoming a foster parent, my hope is that this letter will help you enter in with eyes wide open!

This letter is not shared with a spirit of hype. There are no invisible cheerleaders holding their pom poms in the background, nor is it shared with a long face and stoic silence.

My letter to you is shared in a peaceful "Come as you are—I'm glad you're here—This is important" vibe. I wish we could be in a coffee shop with good background music, cozy chairs, and a warm drink in hand. (I'm partial to coffee mugs half-filled with cream). Know that as you read this letter, I'm leaning forward in my chair, ready to listen and ready to share.

Chapter One

Things to Know Right Out of the Gate

EXPECT THE UNEXPECTED

Foster care is a zig-zaggy road with hairpin turns.

If you like your future path carefully paved before you in a straight, predictable line with plenty of clearly marked signs alerting you to every slight turn around the bend, this fostering journey will be especially difficult. Foster care is rarely predictable. This path will not always not feel efficient. You will likely perceive at times that you are circling around rather than proceeding in a linear, logical way. There will be a few stretches of smooth pavement, and then, without warning, you'll be navigating rough terrain with a sheer cliff that will make your heart drop on one side and a mountain that looks insurmountable on the other.

With my three sons, who all came to me as children needing a foster home (none of whom are biologically related to one another), there have been multiple unexpected detours in each of their stories. With my first child in foster care, who came to me as a toothless first-grader and lived with us for a year, we re-connected after an abrupt good-bye and more than a decade of no contact. He didn't call me Mom then, but he calls me Mom now. He is the "Son of my Heart," a young man in his early 20's who has experienced an unquantifiable amount of trauma.

I developed a significant relationship with my other son's biological mom, who also grew up in foster care. It was awkward and a bit clunky at first and has been filled with a roller-coaster of ups and downs. We've been in each other's lives since 2008. Our relationship has been touted by many, including the judge who terminated her rights, as a head-turning, unexpected collaboration. She, and her other children living with her, are a part of our family, and we've taken the long, winding road to get to where we are today.

My third son is another living example of the unexpected. I was asked if we could pick up him as a newborn from the hospital "for the weekend." That baby stayed with us as his forever family. "For the weekend" and "for forever" are quite different! While those who are open to adoption may consider this a dream scenario, this seemingly healthy newborn has grown into our precious child who, years after the adoption finalized, was diagnosed with irreparable, life-long brain damage due to in-utero alcohol exposure. We fiercely love our son *and* this has unexpectedly set our family on a challenging and unexpected path. This is a massive understatement!

This is the point where I ask between sips of coffee, "Have I freaked you out sharing the brief overview of what the expected fostering road has actually looked like in my own life?" If so, that was not my intention, but for the sake of keeping this thing rolling, know I'm sending you an empathetic nod and a wink.

While I just shared the briefest overview of how saying yes to foster care has led to permanent changes in our family structure, we have also said yes many times to a child or sibling set who have stayed with us for varying lengths of time, transitioning them back to their biological families, adoptive families, or longer-term foster families.

As someone who has been walking this fostering road for a while, I will share with you this foundational truth: if I could have looked into a crystal ball and seen what this fostering road would eventually look and feel like in the roughest part of the road, I might never have had the courage to take that first step. I would have felt overwhelmed and in-over-my-head. Fear—plain and simple—would have made me miss out on knowing these children who needed us and who have come to fill up space in my heart and around my table, whether for a season or a lifetime.

While this book you're holding, *No Sugar-Coating,* is an efficient rundown of high-level considerations when discerning if foster parenting is for you, if you desire to know the background stories and depth of lived experiences which led to the insight in this book, I warmly invite you to pick up a copy of my book *A Love-Stretched Life: Stories on Wrangling Hope, Embracing the Unexpected, and Discovering the Meaning of Family.*

DON'T COUNT YOURSELF OUT

I've encountered some people who self-select out of foster care because they believe they wouldn't qualify due to their housing situation, their relationship status, the fact that they work full-time, or a hiccup in their background. ("I live in an apartment, am single, and I work a weird schedule. I can't foster, can I?" This is what my dear friend, Emily, wondered before she became a foster parent.) If you're willing to move forward with foster care, check to see what your agency requirements are before you assume it's not within the realm of possibility.

Some believe you must have a squeaky-clean background with nothing a tad messy or complicated. In other words, only perfect people need apply. (Would there be anyone fostering on earth if that were the case?) The reality is that people who have some grit in their stories from having to overcome hard things may actually be able to relate better to the kids walking in their door because they are overcomers as well.

Single people, even those with no previous parenting experience, can absolutely foster. I know several who do, and they are, undoubtedly, the foster parent their child needed.

Know that families come in all shapes and sizes and there isn't a one-size-fits-all model for family. Kids need adults who care and will be there for them. It's not about perfection. It's about having eyes wide open to this journey and still being willing.

FEARFUL WONDERINGS

Many people never get past the fear stage in their minds. These foster care waters are tainted with fear. For some, simply the act of beginning to engage the possibility of fostering causes a dam in their mind to come crumbling down; worst case scenarios instantly flood out the possibility.

* How will fostering affect my children?

* Can my marriage sustain what foster care may bring?

* Can I handle what it takes to engage in foster care as a single parent?

* Does my full life allow for taking care of children from hard places?

* What does trauma look like and how will it manifest in my home? What if I can't handle it?

* Could I really love and let go? Would my heart and the well-being of my family ever bounce back?

* What if foster care changes my relationships and my very life as I know it?

These, and so many more, are all good and real questions! Proactively asking questions and feeling a certain amount of caution is healthy. Frankly, I feel a wide-eyed, protective caution when I hear a person expressing nothing but enthusiastic confidence in talking about foster care before ever having lived it. Foster care isn't something you pick up, casually throwing it into your shopping cart, and then proceeding on in life as normal.

If you want to discern if foster care is yours to do in this life, it will require pressing into the fear, listening to those who have walked this road before you, and stepping forward with open ears, eyes, and heart. It is simply human nature to fear the unknown. A curious and cautious fear about how foster care will affect your life is healthy. For many, however, a debilitating fear takes them out from ever truly considering foster care.

DISCERN TOGETHER

If you want to engage in foster care and your partner does not, that means this isn't the time. While it's natural that one person may have more of a keen interest in the beginning of the process, don't proceed if you're dragging the other along. A genuine "Let's start this process and discern together" needs to be expressed from both of you before you buckle your seatbelts for this wild ride.

Right after college, with Spanish as one of my undergrad majors, I headed to a Guatemalan orphanage where I lived as a house parent in a mobile home trailer full of elementary-school-aged girls and taught at the school for six months. After I finished my Masters in Teaching English as a Second Language in California and got married, I brought my husband, Luke, back to Guatemala where I taught English at a private high school and he enrolled in Spanish Language school. On the weekend, we would return to the same orphanage to offer respite relief and let the house parents stay at our apartment in the city. This time together, sharing life with vulnerable kids physically surrounding us at all times, was forever impacting. When my husband and I returned from living in Guatemala for the better part of a year and moved to New York for him to complete his doctoral program, we asked in our mid-twenties, "Where are the vulnerable children here?"

This question led us straight to the doors of foster care, never having known anyone who had fostered before.

While fostering still varies greatly from place to place, in 2003 and with where we were living at the time, foster care was not highlighted as it is today in my community. It was never once mentioned in our faith community and I can't recall ever reading about it or engaging in related conversation about foster care, barring that one lonely poster at the gym.

It goes without saying that there was a genuine need for loving, caring, certified foster parents then, just as there is now. The difference is that now, having walked through the doors of foster care, I can never again claim ignorance.

IMPORTANT TRUTHS

While all of the following points are worthy of a much deeper dive, here are some additional things I want to succinctly share with you so you're in the know. Should you choose to proceed with becoming a certified foster parent, you will learn more about each of these topics in your training class.

* When a child enters foster care, the preference is for the child to be placed with biological relatives. If no willing relatives are available, the second priority is to place children with someone they already know, such as a neighbor, teacher, or family friend. If nobody can be found in either of these preferred categories (sometimes referred to as "kith and kin"), the third choice is turning to strangers (general applicant foster parents). These are people with no previous connection to the child.

* There is an over-representation of youth of color in foster care. It is vital to keep kids connected with their cultural and ethnic identities, as well as learn from experts about important aspects of hair and skin care if their needs are different from your own. (I encourage you to ask your agency about practical resources so you are aware of places and activities to keep your child's heritage connections strong).

* The national median age of a child in foster care is 9 years old. Most children enter foster care with siblings. If there are not enough spaces in a home for siblings to stay together, or if, for example, the foster home only takes in elementary-school-aged children and there is an infant as part of the sibling set, they are often split into various foster homes. This, needless to say, is highly traumatic. It's possible that children in foster care may be even more bonded to their siblings than they are to their parents, given the effects of trauma.

* Foster care is intended to be temporary. The length of stay for a child in foster care varies greatly depending on many factors. In my home state of Oregon, the median state average is 18 months. In Oregon, about 60% of children entering foster care are reunited with their biological families (with

the remaining 40% being split into adoption (17%), guardianship (12%) aging out (5%) and other smaller, more detailed categories).[1] I encourage you to check out and ask about the specific statistics in your state.

1 Oregon DHS Child Welfare Data Book 2018

Chapter Two

As You Begin Foster Care

KNOW YOUR "WHY"

People are already familiar with the headline zingers of atrocities committed against children in foster care, mugshots of abusive foster parents, and million-dollar lawsuits. What the community needs to hear more of is your humble "why." What compels you to engage and take this road less-traveled? Be prepared to clearly articulate your reason for stepping into this because folks will inevitably ask.

In my dining room, I see this meaningful, hand-made gift from a friend. On a wooden sign in simple white letters is written:

> *Do Justice. Walk Humbly. Love Mercy.*
> Micah 6:8

Every time I look at it, I am reminded that in spite of what we see around us, I am invited to show up in this world in real, earnest ways. Through loving my neighbor I am open to being changed through my experiences. I believe every human being has innate God-given value and worth and bears the image of the Divine. What has been true in the past and continues to be true every day is that I always have more to learn and further to go in being transformed into a kind, wise person who extends grace. Opportunity for growth comes to me through being in relationship with others, many of whom have walked a markedly different path than my own. This is not just seeing other people and rubbing shoulders for a short conversation, but walking beside them and allowing the truth of their life and experience, so different from my own, to transform me through the privilege of being in relationship.

I don't want all this relationship talk to sound like a Hallmark commercial. We all know relationships are tricky, often with no quick fixes, but it's true that faith is at the center of my "why" for engaging in the plethora of relationships foster care brings.

Things in foster care are rarely black and white. The reason for this is that foster care is a bleak world of gray, exposing the complexities and heartache of this world. In the midst of the anguish, foster care has invited me to dive into a world of brilliant vibrancy as I witness and engage in the kaleidoscope of colorful pain and joy up close, swirled and blended together.

Some people's "why" may be rooted in their faith. Others may start forging this path after hearing about the overwhelming need for more foster homes in their neighborhood. For others it may be a sense of rescue. *"I'm going to save a child from a terrible situation and work hard to give him a nice life."* My personal, initial "why" in 2003 likely had a combination of all of these elements.

If an adrenaline rush, a swoop of rescuing compassion, and a sole scripture verse is the driver of what is pressing you into foster care, don't proceed. It may be enough to get you through the certification classes and get a child to walk through your front door, but it will not take you much further. Foster care will surely invite you to dig deep into your personal "why"—whatever that may be—and to develop some grit and tenacity to hold steadfast.

Contrary to the images you have heard, being a foster parent does not ask you to sound the trumpet, gallop onto the scene on horseback, and save the day. It's a quiet invitation to intentionally open wide your front door to kids whose lives have gone awry through no fault of their own. Kids need many things, but chief among them are safety, security, and someone who won't give up on them. The commitment to show up and be steadfast lays a foundation for developing trust. In good times and in bad, this takes courage.

Courage:

* *the ability to do something that frightens one*
* *strength in the face of pain or grief*

CHECK YOUR HERO CAPE AT THE DOOR

When community members hear you're stepping into foster care, prepare yourself to have puffed-up hero comments bestowed upon you. The community will crown you with the image of a harrowing rescuer, like a superhero action figure. That is, after all, a far more alluring picture than an ordinary person with strengths and weaknesses who chooses perseverance in the midst of fear.

Be aware that the hero comments you will undoubtedly hear do not come with an invisible cape to tie around your neck. You are not signing up to live out a narrative of rescue with cartoon bubble captions that say "POW" in the life of a vulnerable child. These comments will not come with secret powers to suddenly empower you to feel the "brave" others will claim you to be. If you rely on the hype to encourage you, you'll soon feel lonely and disillusioned.

No matter whether you choose to make your voice strong to advocate or speak in a whisper while trying to comfort a distraught child, you will have plenty of opportunity on this fostering road to exhibit a very ordinary, one-foot-in-front-of-the-other type of courage.

BE BOTH REALISTIC AND FLEXIBLE ABOUT WHO TO PARENT

There is a myth prospective foster parents have that once they're in the system as foster parents, they're at the mercy of saying yes to whomever they are called about—from infant to teen—with varying levels of need. This is simply not true! At some point within the certification process, you will talk with someone at your agency about the particulars. I would encourage you to think intentionally about who (gender and age range of a child or sibling group) would be the best fit for your family and the behaviors you are currently prepared to handle.

Remember, there is no invisible superhero cape on this journey. The tension you'll hold on this journey is that sometimes your heart and desire to say yes will outweigh your capacity for you and your family to take on all that yes requires. Saying yes from a sense of guilt or a swoop of divine compassion will not sustain you if that yes supersedes your daily ability.

My friend Kara was sure that she only wanted to open up her home to toddlers. She did so, and it was harder than she expected for many reasons. Then Kara got a call for a 12-year-old girl, and after weighing the pros and cons, she decided to flex. In doing that, she discovered this child was the best fit for her family, including her three younger boys. While many foster parents go with the conventional wisdom of not taking in children older than their youngest, there are plenty of families like Kara's that have switched up the birth order. It's a highly personal choice. The general line of thinking for those who choose to take in children younger than their youngest usually has to do with wanting their kids to be their influencers and not the ones influenced. I encourage you to seek out the experiences of other foster parents and ask how they've discerned this birth order conversation and what their experience has been.

New foster parents often express a real hesitation to say no initially because they're afraid they may not be called again. This is not true. The sad reality is that even if you say no to this child, there may very well be another desperate call from your agency, asking about the possible fit of a different child. This call may come in the next week, a few days, or even a few hours later. Most foster parents have walked the tightrope of intentionally discerning beforehand *and* being flexible simultaneously as they discern yes or no.

DEPRESSING MATH IN MOST COMMUNITIES

Don't be surprised if you discuss with your agency that a girl aged 5-10 would be the best fit for your family and your agency calls, asking you to consider fostering an 11-year-old boy. What's up with that? Are they purposely trying to steamroll your boundaries? They are not. This is where we realize that the core of foster care is about finding a family for a waiting child, not a family waiting to hand-pick a child. It's a subtle but colossal difference!

In most communities, the number of certified foster homes is significantly less than the number of kids needing a foster family. The math simply doesn't add up. The agency's hands are then tied in striving to make a strategic placement match. In an ideal scenario, a family's unique abilities are matched with a child's specific needs. Too often, however, agencies are left scrambling trying to simply get a roof—any roof—over a child's head. Not being able to make intentional, strategic placement matches sets the family up for a higher probability of burnout and increases the likelihood that the child may need to move on to another foster home. This will, sadly, be the norm until our nation has more foster parents waiting for the opportunity to foster, rather than a child waiting for a foster home.

You will inevitably get that fated call from your agency, and you will recognize either a hint or overt desperation in the caller's voice, asking if you'd consider fostering Jordan and Samantha. Again, I encourage you to think intentionally *before* that call about your parenting capabilities. There are times to stick with your spoken, pre-discerned boundaries and not waver, even though it can feel heavy to hang up the phone after saying no. And yet, even with stated boundaries, there's a fair amount of just going with your gut and being open.

ANTICIPATE THE ENTOURAGE

When you begin to foster, you're not just welcoming in a child, but many others tethered to him. Among them are professionals from the agency who need to meet with you at various times— weekly, monthly, and bi-annually. Children in foster care also come with an attorney, appointments with counselors, mental health and medical professionals, school meetings, and court dates attached to them. So, while you may be welcoming one child, there are many support people and services in place attached to that child, which will require more time set aside for meetings and appointments.

CREATE EXTRA MARGINS OF EMOTIONAL SPACE AND TIME

Before a child comes into your home, make a list of what energizes you and post it in a place where you'll be reminded each day that engaging in one of these activities isn't selfish. It is a preservation lifeline. Take a good look at your calendar to see where you can schedule some alone time and one-on-one time with your family members. This time can also include special time with your child in foster care. Knowing that there will be undivided attention given to all members of the household can assuage some of the highs and lows of adjusting to this "new normal" family dynamic. Sometimes the new dynamic can simply feel like "too much"—*Too much noise, too much commotion, too much drama, too much whining—just too much!*

We had one child sit at our table and never stop talking. Ever. Every night it was one run-on sentence crashing into the next; verbal processing, stream of consciousness talking to the extreme. He did this for the entire meal. In a non-shaming way, still expressing interest in all he had to share, we tried to model for him how a family conversation works around the dinner table, a concept entirely foreign to him. I understood it better when the psychologist helped me see that he might be doing this because it's his own way of affirming to himself that he's there and present. He literally needed to speak his existence into the world to know his presence. And while I felt compassion for this child and the sad "why" behind this, I also saw my kids' eyes glaze over and look downward during family meals.

Don't wait for potential "too-much-ness" to wear your family down. Have a concrete plan in place in advance for what you will do to create equilibrium and meet the emotional needs of everyone under your roof, yourself included.

THE "EXTRA" OF FOSTER CARE

It can feel thrilling and exhilarating to be on the same page of doing something significant with your partner. Investing in the life of a vulnerable child by welcoming her in your home is significant. And yet, the high-level, cognitive ascension of "being on the same page" when doing something significant together will likely not be enough to allow your relationship to weather all the "extra" that foster care brings (extra emotions, extra relationships to navigate both inside and outside the home, extra appointments for the child, etc.). All this "extra" can quickly lead to a huge strain without intentional time to process. Writing this time on your calendar and protecting it is a good first step for both individuals and couples. Many foster parents I know, myself included, have benefited from proactively seeking out an individual therapist, marriage counselor, or Spiritual Director to help weather the storm brought on by the "extra" of foster care, which is often difficult to quantify.

HOW FOSTER CARE HAS AFFECTED MY KIDS

There's almost nothing we as a society hold more sacred than the lives we've carefully constructed for ourselves and our families. When foster care potentially threatens to change our life dynamics, it's understandable that there are big questions. In fact, there should be big questions! After all, this isn't the game of LIFE where you spin the wheel, add a peg to the backseat of your plastic car, and continue on your merry way. If you're seriously considering foster care, isn't it reasonable to want to know the answer to the question, *"How will this affect my biological kids?"*

I've found that for many people, their fears turn first to questions surrounding the impact of foster care on the family, specifically their biological kids.

This journey has made my biological kids other-centered in a compassionate way that could never have been taught by a character study alone. They have an understanding that the worst thing in this world isn't some disappointment such as having to choose which birthday party to attend because they were invited to two at the same time.

Opening our front door to children in need has brought a keen level of awareness to our children beyond their years. These aren't just invisible children in foster care somewhere out there. They are Grace, Lucy, Kevin, Stanford, Jorge, Bella, Skylar, Noah, and others whose faces and stories are seated around our table. My children were aware from a young age that some moms and dads are not able to make safe choices for themselves and therefore can't keep their kids safe. They realize that some adults are not kind to those they are supposed to protect.

Over the years I have seen many examples of my kids engaging others with sensitivity and kindness, which I do believe foster care has helped ingrain in them. This includes my teenage daughter doing a school project to prevent the bullying of kids with invisible disabilities. Another daughter moved seats to intentionally sit with the child sitting alone in the cafeteria. My son went above and beyond to extend a warm welcome to the new kid in class for whom English was his second language. While there are no halos over my kids' heads (and I could easily share examples of sibling rivalry around here), I am grateful when I notice them compassionately engaging others.

FOSTER CARE PRICKS THE BUBBLE

It may be eye-opening and upsetting for some kids living in a safe family to learn that not all parents are safe and healthy. For many families with younger kids, stepping into foster care can be seen as pricking the protective bubble of the reality we strive so hard to set up for our children. Most people don't associate the whole-some goodness of children riding their bikes out in the cul-de-sac on a sunny day with sitting them down and having a conversa-tion about why kids enter foster care. There's a natural tendency to want to protect our children and shut out anything perceived as distressing.

We've found, however, that in talking about this reality in age-ap-propriate ways, we can expand the layers of understanding as our kids go from toddlers to elementary school to high school. Our kids will take in this reality and take their cues from how we ap-proach it. Of course, as our kids grow older, we have the privilege of seeing and listening to the myriad of ways that foster care has affected them.

"NEW NORMAL"

It wouldn't be fair for me to talk about the character-shaping as-pects of engaging in foster care without being honest about the real sacrifice. While I could share about resilience formed in my children through foster care, there are challenging aspects as well.

One of the toughest family factors, for kids and parents alike, is to adjust to a "new normal" as family dynamics ebb and flow with every hello and good-bye.

A common challenge is for the family to witness the manifes-tation of what trauma looks like behaviorally for others now sharing their home. For some children in foster care, there is a discrepancy between their chronological age and developmen-tal age. For example, a child may be 9 years old in calendar years but may behave in ways that resemble that of a 5-year-old. The reasons for this often include in-utero substance exposure and trauma. For foster parents, giving cognitive assent to this real-ity and having an action plan of how to engage it are separate things. Many foster parents will share with you that traditional parenting strategies fall short. Parents and children alike may feel bewildered and biological children may take note of how "unfair" things may be or that the child is "getting away with things." Foster parents have the incredibly difficult privilege of trying to cull forth their child in foster care's highest level of capability while also taking into account what is a realistic standard for that child. Of course, this doesn't apply to all children in foster care, but it certainly applies when talking about challenging family dynamics.

Another common challenge in establishing a "new normal" is children needing to share their parents' time with the new child in foster care (who comes with many needs and a lot of appointments). The high needs of children in foster care may mean that parenting attention isn't split up evenly between the number of children in the home.

As a parent, I value my children feeling that their voice matters and that engaging in foster care as a family has significance, not simply a choice that's being made for them. While it doesn't negate the importance of being intentional with your children and taking into account their feelings, it adds perspective to consider that kids have to enter foster care each and every day with no choice in the matter.

One way we strive for balance is to intentionally create space to hear our children's thoughts. We check in with them about how we can show them that we love and value them while opening up our home to kids in foster care. This may look like taking them to school late so we can have a one-on-one breakfast. It may look like turning off the TV in the evenings to have an intentional family conversation. The point is that we want to push our children to have a welcoming eye for "the other" without driving them well past a point of goodwill and creating resentment. It can be a tricky balance.

Families want to experience harmony. It's true that with every willing yes to welcome a child in foster care into your home, there's an unbounded opportunity to fold in, love, and help to heal. What's equally true is that with every yes, there's the very real possibility that your family can be thrown into disequilibrium, especially if the behavioral, emotional, and supervisory needs of the children you welcome are more than what you initially anticipated. Of course, these needs are not the fault of the kids you welcome. Maladaptive coping and survival skills due to the trauma of what happened to them before they ever walked in your front door will most likely be something you will encounter. Children don't end up in foster care without reason.

Chapter Three

In the Midst of Your Foster Care Journey

COMFORT FOOD

Always keep boxes of mac 'n' cheese, a cake mix, and birthday candles stashed away in your cupboards. It's important kids have comfort food they are familiar with, especially right at the beginning. Let up on the "eat your broccoli" battle as kids adjust to being in your home. For a child in my home who lived in a car since toddlerhood and only ate fast or convenience store food, even eating with a utensil was a new experience! Introducing healthy foods they may be unfamiliar with will take time and encouragement. The likelihood is high, as I've experienced several times, that you will have a child who will walk in your door and whisper that it was her birthday three days ago. With some gentle question-asking, you may learn there wasn't a single acknowledgment. Trust me that if you're willing to receive a call, press through the fear and answer with a "yes," you won't ever regret throwing mac 'n' cheese, corn dogs, chips, a cake mix, and candles in your grocery cart. Keep a small stockpile of comfort food

in your home. We can increase kids' comfort during an uncom-
fortable time by having these items on hand as we are simultaneously mindful to introduce new foods.

EXPECT HEAVY THINGS, EVEN IN THE LIGHTER MOMENTS

For kids who have experienced abuse and neglect, their sharing
of a past experience may come up at any random point in time.
For you and me as adults, sharing may only happen when it's quiet, we're in the presence of a trusted friend, and have a drink in
front of us. With children, however, you can never predict when
there will be something important revealed, even in the midst of
the hubbub of a normal day.

I recall providing respite care for a foster parent friend of ours
and said yes to having her blond-haired, blue-eyed, five-year-old
foster daughter for the weekend. As all my kids with their messy
bed heads sat around the kitchen table with bowls of cereal in
front of them, Hannah said, almost cheerfully, "Do you know
my daddy died?" Being a close friend and in the inner circle of
trust with this foster parent, I knew that her dad drowned when
he was high, running away from authorities, and jumped off a
downtown bridge.

One of my girls got out of her chair and gave Hannah a little side
hug. The other one said, "I'm sorry, Hannah. That's so sad your
dad died." I added my own acknowledgement of this statement.
Hannah continued to spoon Cheerios in her mouth, munch
away, and then mid-chew with milk spilling down her chin, she
announced loudly, "AND he was eaten by SHARKS!" At this, all
my kids' eyes widened as they looked at me. Sweet Hannah gave
a classic example of kids sharing the reality of what they believe
to be true thrown into the everyday normalcy of breakfast on a
Saturday morning.

While there can be overly dramatic moments, the less-than dramatic can also leave me wide-eyed with the re-telling of a traumatic experience.

The Son of my Heart who was the first child to ever walk through my door in foster care at age six, and with whom I reconnected after over a decade of zero contact, had two divots in his knee. I asked him what happened. He told me of being released from incarceration, being homeless, and being shot—twice—in the leg. He was in the hospital for two weeks with no visitors and was then released back to the streets on probation. He said this in the way you or I may mundanely talk about what we plan to eat for lunch.

A good friend of mine and stellar foster dad shared with me that while driving his teen daughter in foster care around town, she looked out the window and calmly and straight-forwardly told him about being raped in the place they had just driven by. While he wanted to have a "Stop the World" moment, she appeared nonchalant as she continued listening to the radio. This would be a later conversation with her therapist.

Vehicles, interestingly, are often a place where things are disclosed. There is very little eye contact required which may feel safer, and if youth are in the same community where they lived before entering foster care, seeing familiar places can evoke memories.

The following are questions preschool and elementary-aged children have asked me or foster parent friends of mine in the everyday fullness of life:

Do people here get locked in closets?
Will this nightlight protect me from the bad man?
Did I lose my food?
Are you going to hit me?

Whether you are sitting at the breakfast table, asking a seemingly mundane question, or driving around, you too will experience heavier things, even in lighter moments.

DO YOUR HOMEWORK ON TRAUMA

I can't recommend highly enough learning about ACES (Adverse Childhood Experiences Study) and the impact of trauma, neglect, and abuse over a lifetime in the body and the brain. Additionally, while the body's primary trauma responses of "flight, fight, or freeze" are usually covered in your foster parenting training, less talked about, but nevertheless real, are the immense effects of secondary trauma.

Secondary trauma is a significant emotional stressor that may occur when an individual hears about the firsthand trauma experiences of others. Secondary trauma may also be talked about as Compassion Fatigue. It's important to know that one can be more susceptible to secondary trauma if they have a personal history with trauma. You can suffer secondary trauma from seeing individuals coping with their own reactions to trauma or from direct contact with children's traumatic stories and behaviors. Friends, please re-read that last sentence! I want you to brace yourself and be prepared. The most common reasons a child enters foster care are physical abuse, sexual abuse, psychological abuse, neglect, domestic violence, incarceration of a parent, a parent's drug and alcohol abuse, or untreated mental illness. If a child is removed from her family, no matter how young, there is loss and trauma, with varying degrees of ripple effects. As the child gets older, there may be ever-emerging ways the trauma resurfaces and needs to be addressed with professional help.

Secondary trauma can have physical, behavioral, and emotional warning signs. While I encourage you to do a deeper dive into this as there are long lists of things that may indicate you are experiencing secondary trauma, some examples include exhaustion, headache, anger, irritability, apathy, over or under eating, and either hypersensitivity or insensitivity to emotionally-charged situations.

Secondary trauma is something foster parents experience and it needs to be talked about more often. Foster care has the uncanny ability to expose your own baggage as you navigate trauma, stories, and behaviors interlaced in the everyday, ordinary moments of life.

KIDS WILL HAVE TRIGGERS; YOU WILL TOO!

Sometimes your well-intentioned heart will be shoved right back in your face by a child who appears to be not even remotely receptive to what you are offering. Know that the way you respond at times to certain situations—even internally—may surprise you. None of us are super-human. Many triggers stem from things in our own background around sight, sound, smell, touch, and taste.

My friend served her child in foster care oatmeal, only for the child to have an immediate melt-down rage. Unbeknownst to my friend, there was significant trauma in the child's home where she was fed oatmeal, and the sight and smell of the oatmeal triggered immediate hysterics. This then interacted with my friend's own trigger of hearing incessant screaming, reminding him of his parents fighting growing up. This also triggered anxiety from the internalized societal norms of what's considered acceptable child-like behavior.

One of my sons often moans "No" and loudly stomps in the house when things don't go his way. Slamming doors is also his thing. While far from the most exasperating behavior in our household, it grates on me significantly, and I know the reason why. Knowing this and naming this helps me not to overreact. There was a time in which I would be escalated, heartbeat racing, curtly telling him to stop it, and at times, barging in right after a door slam, not modeling what I needed to be doing myself. Though I'm far from perfect, I have come a long way in the importance of talking calmly and quietly, and when safety issues are not present, giving space and circling back around at a time when his mind and body can receive input.

Knowing secondary trauma and triggers are real, consider counseling for yourself as you begin this journey. The better you know yourself and recognize the triggers in your story that will collide and potentially explode with the behavioral triggers of children, the better off and healthier everyone will be.

SUSTAIN YOURSELF

It can be difficult when we feel like we're giving endlessly and getting nothing back. It can be even more difficult when we're being met with defiance, name-calling, or aggression. It's easy to think, "I signed up to welcome a vulnerable child, but I did not sign up for *this.*"

This is where a standing walk, time in nature, a prayer or gratitude journal, or a coffee date with someone who "gets it" without having to explain all the nitty-gritty details will be a lifeline. These are life-giving to me. Think about what energizes you.

Remember the basic principles of being healthy, which can be easy to cognitively remember and hard to implement. As I share this next sentence, know I'm preaching to myself here, too. Getting sufficient sleep (though I'm well acquainted with many reasons why this may be challenging), eating nutritious food, and hydrating will serve you well anytime. It will especially serve you well while engaging all the extra complexities of foster care.

When our foster son came to us at 6 months old with only four days notice, I had a fairly full spring schedule already in the works with things I'd committed to lead or participate in where others were counting on me. Because I didn't birth this child, I just figured I could welcome him, engage in changing family dynamics, and keep all my balls of commitment in the air. I look back on that time and wished I'd slowed down. If you've ever brought a baby home from the hospital and know the margin you put around yourself and your family during that time, that's a good place to start. Nobody has an expectation that you'll come home from the hospital and continue right along as before and attend that Tuesday night book club and Friday morning volunteering without skipping a beat. You should extend yourself the same margin as you welcome children in foster care. Even if you're sleeping through the night and the child at your door is in fourth grade, create a protective bubble where you give yourself a wide margin to adjust.

LEARN WHAT IS UNIQUE ABOUT EVERY CHILD

"Foster" is not an adjective that implies kids are the same.

Despite the stereotype, remember that not all children in foster care have an outward manifestation of high needs. Some children develop typically and in remarkably healthy ways despite all they've endured. At the same time, just because a child isn't outwardly exhibiting concerning behaviors, this does not mean that the trauma responsible for them entering foster care is somehow solved and doesn't need to be intentionally addressed.

For some children, having you to invest in them with patience and compassion will be enough to learn new behavioral patterns, help rewire healing in their brain, and feel their inherent worth. For others, the notion of "overcoming" whatever led them to initially walk through your door in the first place will be a lifelong dance of two steps forward, three steps back. Finally, for others still, there will be nothing "seasonal" about their high needs and maladaptive behaviors. There may be hurdles they will never jump over in life. Trauma can cripple a person's self-worth and purpose.

It's important to note that with one child, you may feel an instant connection. With another, it may slowly build over time, and there are times you may never actually feel a deep connection. This may feel confusing, but this doesn't mean you're a bad parent. With some children, you may feel devastated to say goodbye, and with others, you may feel relieved. Go easy on yourself. Regardless of warm, fuzzy feelings, we can all agree that all children are worthy of feeling the foundational safety of belonging.

Chapter Four

Let's Talk Community

PREPARE YOURSELF FOR A PLETHORA OF COMMENTS ABOUT FOSTER CARE!

"I get it!"

Brace yourself, it's just a matter of time before that one lady will inevitably come up and tell you with all sincerity that she knows *"exactly"* what foster care is like because she babysat her friend's dog for several weeks, got attached, and shed a tear when she said good-bye. Or the woman who, seated at a round table at a church event, leans over and whispers, "I foster stray cats. I *get* it!"

There was a time when a comment like this would tip my internal, non-gracious "Are you KIDDING me?" meter right over the top. Now I can hold that tension and muster a calm, grace-filled response, which usually includes a head nod (*I'm not gonna tell you why I'm smiling at your ridiculous comparison*) and then taking the high road and pivoting the conversation where I want it to land: "Working with our community's most vulnerable children in foster care has been life-changing for me." And leaving it at that.

While you want to be authentic, there is only so much emotional energy one can expend in a day, and you have to save it for those who have a genuine willingness to hear about your experience. Uninformed comments here and there by people who are not regularly in your life may not be worth the emotional energy. By all means, however, educate them graciously if you have the capacity to do so.

"I'd get too attached!"

It's also just a matter of time before a well-intentioned person will learn you're a foster parent, clutch their hand to their heart and proclaim, "Oh! I could never do that. I'd get way too attached!"

If you think you will cry when a child leaves because you'd be attached to them, congratulations, you may be a great candidate for the privilege of this difficult road less traveled. A child in foster care has likely already walked the road of having a caregiver that can't be fully present or attach, often due to substance abuse, untreated mental illness, domestic violence, or incarceration. Now it's time for a new path. Attaching yourself in healthy ways to your children in foster care is exactly what's needed for their healthy development.

"My heart would break!"

This common sentiment feeds into the over-protective notion that it's all about *me* and *my* heart over offering a child a safe home who needs one. I'm not advocating that you immediately velcro your whole heart to a child the instant they walk in the door, but what I am suggesting is that if someone is an emotionally healthy adult, a vulnerable child's need for attachment trumps a healthy adult's needs for protection from potential heartbreak.

"You're an Angel!"

In the midst of summoning ordinary courage to foster, you will have plenty of halo comments thrown your way by well-meaning encouragers. Someone I know chooses to respond by simply saying, "Ask those who live with me and see if they agree with you on that."

"They're so lucky to have you!"

Let's get one thing straight. Kids in foster care are not lucky. The fact that they had someone who had to stand in for a caregiver who could not keep them safe is not lucky. It's perfectly fine for people to express, "I'm so glad these children are safe and well-cared for by you." We all know that, sadly, this cannot be said about all foster homes, but a child being safe and well-cared for in a foster home should not require a four-leaf clover. It's best to be intentional about language and leave luck out of it.

"Wow! They're foster kids? They're so _____."

Another standard line to brace yourself for is "I can't believe they're foster kids. They're so _____(Fill in the blank with "adorable, smart, clean, polite," etc.). It's as if the very adjective "foster" implies ugliness, unintelligence, and filth. For this reason, I make every conscious effort to say "child in foster care" rather than "foster kid." This phrasing emphasizes first and foremost that they are children who are in this situation because of the inability of a caregiver to properly keep them safe. They are children who never were asked if they wanted to be taken into foster care. It was a choice made for them.

"Oh! He doesn't look like you!"

My friend who is a single foster parent with naturally blonde hair shared that in the aisle of a grocery store someone stared at her baby, caught her eye and uttered, "I expected a blonde baby in your cart." The baby clearly did not look like her. In that state-ment, my friend felt both a subtle sense of disapproval as she followed the gaze of this stranger checking out her hand for a wedding ring. It was also a mini invitation for an explanation as to why the Samoan baby was sitting in her cart. This scene has been repeated in multiple contexts with multiple kids of friends of mine. You are welcome to give a response (while respecting the privacy of the child, especially to strangers in public places), but remember this too: You don't owe any explanation to a strang-er's curious questioning. It's perfectly fine to nod and literally roll on through.

"God won't give you more than you can handle."

When things are tough, well-meaning people may attempt to en-courage you with this statement. It is highly likely on this fos-tering journey that you *will* be given more than what you feel like you can handle. The same goes for "God gives special kids to special people." These comments end up making those receiving them feel isolated rather than encouraged.

"You signed up for this!"

While it is indeed true that you signed up, it doesn't mean that you are not entitled to feel emotions along the way or a need to ask for help. In talking with foster parents, this is one of the most hurtful phrases a foster parent can hear in a time of trial. The implied message here is that since a person signed up, they shouldn't need support or have emotions in a trying time.

LITTLE ORPHAN ANNIE EYE TWINKLE

Often, when I meet with prospective foster parents, they have what I have personally deemed the "Little Orphan Annie" twinkle in their eye. They have loving hearts, ready and willing to pour out, and they have all the amenities that most children would adore. Some even have big houses and yards that look like they're straight out of a magazine and they take fancy family vacations. They may inwardly be tempted to think that a child will feel immense gratitude to live a "from rags to riches" storyline.

Some, even without those enviable extras, may be tempted to believe that consistent food, clothing, and shelter, when a child may have never experienced those foundational pillars of security, will be things that produce an ever-flowing fountain of expressed thankfulness.

It won't.

Exactly how many times as a child did you profusely, verbally, thank your parents for feeding you, clothing you, and giving you shelter? While helping kids develop manners that will serve them well in life is one thing, there should never be an expectation for a child to grovel in gratitude over the basics of felt safety.

THE IMPORTANCE OF FRIENDSHIPS WITH OTHER FOSTER PARENTS

Don't go at it alone. In a culture that prizes self-sufficiency as one of our highest values, this can be tough for some. It's not a matter, however, of *if* the going gets tough. It's simply a matter of *when*.

Think critically about who your support people are and plainly ask if they're willing to walk alongside you as you foster. Identify a village by way of a few caring people who will link arms, prop you up, and encourage you. Ideally, this village will include both foster parents and those who are not fostering.

This journey will change you. This is your one take-it-to-the-bank guarantee of stepping into foster care. And this guarantee can be for better or worse.

For worse, if you're not surrounded by like-minded others, this journey can make you bitter. It can make you self-righteous, feel judgmental of others who have not chosen this same path, and give you "Martyr Syndrome." *"Oh? You're going on vacation again? Don't worry about me. I'll be right here taking care of our community's most vulnerable children!"*

For better, this foster care journey transforms you into a more compassionate person who can simultaneously hold the tension of beauty and the brokenness of all that should not be in the life of a child.

There is much to be said for having other foster parents who have walked the same path and "get it" as a core part of your village. Without having to explain, they will know the sorrow and the privilege of what it's like to be up all night rocking a baby that is yours just for a season, the behavioral roller-coaster of emotions that often occur after a visit with a biological parent, what it may feel like to see the principal's name and number buzz your personal cell, or hear the heart-piercing statement of "My mom doesn't love me" spoken by a sorrowful first grader.

For foster parents navigating rugged terrain, there's much comfort in a knowing glance or a nod of acknowledgement from others who get it when no explanation of grief or loss is needed. It alleviates our isolation to personally know others who can't be out past 7 pm because of the meltdown that will ensue, or the feeling of victory that comes from making a Target run with a child staying buckled in her seatbelt. Foster parents are able to celebrate what many would consider a low-level, age-appropriate, behavioral expectation. They see up close the shaky starting line or hairpin detours in life that kids are sometimes handed through no fault of their own. Foster parents can commiserate about court, the system, and using their sacred voice to advocate for voiceless children.

BUILD YOUR VILLAGE AND INCLUDE THOSE
NOT FOSTERING

As you appreciate the camaraderie of other foster parents, it's equally important to be balanced. Stay open to inviting others who are not fostering to come alongside you. Stave off pride and allow others to help you when they offer to bring a meal, pick up something at the store, or help with laundry. To quote a dear friend who put it a bit more bluntly, "Get over yourself and accept help!" If people offer you general support such as "Let me know how I can help," take them up on it with some concrete suggestions. Your willingness to be open and show others raw glimpses of the beauty and pain in this journey will be their humble invitation to be a part of a story larger than themselves. It may make them allies.

Of course, you can't let everyone who expresses an interest in what you're doing join your circle, so think critically about your capacity. It will take investment, time, and gentle explanations, but if you're not willing to do so, it's not fair to write others off as "not getting it," as I've seen some veteran foster parents express. Others' understanding about foster care will stem from their connection with you. This connection depends on your willingness to open up your life and have deep friendships with those not fostering.

I belong to a dinner club which meets every other month. I'm the only foodie imposter, but they still let me in because I enjoy talking with the women around the table. When it was my turn to host last month, I ditched my initial thought of getting a take-and-bake pizza and instead impressed everyone with overcooked, rubbery chicken. I should have gone with my original idea! I have never laughed, cried, and felt so connected to a group of women who were once virtual strangers, but are now dear friends simply through gathering around the table with a regular rhythm.

They know the bullet points of my fostering journey and occasionally request updates or ask thoughtful questions, but we don't often talk about foster care when we meet together, which I appreciate. I need friends and spaces where fostering isn't the main connection.

Feeling overwhelmed is not exclusive to parenting vulnerable children, though it's true that there are many unique aspects of this foster journey that create a high likelihood for "overwhelm" being a part of your journey. As foster parents engage with trauma first-hand and the enormously challenging behaviors that manifest from loss, there may be times they feel that they're taking on more than their fair share of hurt in the world. This is normal. Over the years, I've had to remind myself that despite how things may appear on the outside, everyone with whom I interact is carrying around invisible burdens.

While foster care may strengthen your relationship with some, do not be surprised if the uniqueness of this journey oppositely affects some friendships. As a foster parent friend put it, "Life became messy with foster care, and I wasn't prepared for some relationships—friends and family alike—to be impacted, but they have been. Some have expressed a lack of understanding and support, which comes across as judgement. This has left me feeling isolated."

A WORD ABOUT SUPPORT GROUPS & MENTORS

Life-giving and in-person support groups for foster parents are hard to find. If you find a supportive, thriving group, you've found a gem! A healthy support group will have a clear facilitator where foster parents are allowed to check in and confidentially share where they are at in relation to the child, themselves, and the direction of the case.

Many foster parent support groups are online. While it's important to have an inner circle group in which you can share all emotions, be aware that unmoderated online support groups tend to be a vortex for the negative. People who may not phrase things so angrily in person vent through a keyboard and then hit "send." While you may feel support from online groups, keep a watchful eye for this tendency. The last thing you need is for your shoulders to droop reading stories and comments full of big emotions and frustrations related to foster care, especially from people you don't know personally.

Expectations and requirements vary from public to private organizations and from state to state. You'll quickly find that there may be a certain way things are outlined on paper, and another way they are lived out in reality. Ask to be matched with a mentor who is more experienced and can help you learn the ropes.

A NEW VOCAB WORD

Foster care is full of acronyms. I can list dozens of insider-talk acronyms from my state and organization. You'll soon learn the lingo of your state and organization, and I'm telling you, it can feel like speaking a different language at times.

Now I'm not one for exclusive, insider-talk, but there are some dynamics that only another foster parent will fully understand. Sometimes the too-much-ness of this journey may get to you, and you may find yourself throwing your hands up in the air and chuckling about something that is truly sad and upsetting; something that others wouldn't react to in the same way, out of self-preservation. The brilliant word I want to introduce you to is this: "hilarisad." It's a combination of both hilarious and sad that encompasses both adjectives simultaneously. When something is so completely sad at its core, but there's also a tinge of humor, it's "hilarisad." A quick-witted friend of mine made this word up on the spot after we learned that a Child-Welfare-involved parent we'd been rooting for tried to rob a corn dog food truck, squirting the ketchup bottle during the hold-up. That's an example of "hilarisad." You now have full permission to insert this new word into your vocabulary. Please note: This is *never* making fun of people, and just a word to describe the reaction one might have about a situation in which these two adjectives are simultaneously present.

Chapter Five

Foster Parenting & The Child's Biological Family

BIOLOGICAL PARENTS & THE "US VS. THEM" DYNAMIC

Perhaps right from the beginning or over time, an "Us vs. Them" mindset may develop with the biological parents. You may not start out that way, but without intentionality, it's easy to become jaded and for this slippery slope narrative to creep in.

If a child has explosive behaviors in your home, it may be tempting to blame the biological parents. (*He clearly struggles in this way because of his biological parents and what they did or didn't do for him*). While there may be some truth to your statement, exasperation and blame are neither productive nor solution-driven.

Many foster parent training courses will mention having a relationship with birth parents, but they don't usually give concrete relational "how-tos". Rarely are the natural fears existing on both sides of this parenting aisle mentioned. By neglecting to encourage this relational dynamic, however, we're missing out on potentially living a more holistic foster care narrative that extends beyond the child.

REACHING OUT

The reality is, if there's a foundational possibility for a relationship to be built, it will take a bit of intrinsic motivation to reach out to one another. Some programs offer a formal introductory program between the foster and biological parent, but I have yet to experience this. Often, you're on your own. If you're willing to reach out in small ways, the foster parent is best suited to initiate contact because of the perceived power differential.

This may feel awkward in the beginning, but a little humanity—a note, eye contact, a handshake, and when appropriate, a hug—can go a long way in calming fears.

GOOD/BAD NARRATIVE & OVERT COMMUNICATION

If we're not intentional to present our humanity to biological parents, we can feed into the "good parent/bad parent" narrative without realizing it. This is, after all, the natural setup of the foster care system. "I'm removing Johnny from you (*bad parent*) and I'm placing him with you (*good parent*)." Nobody ever says it like this, of course, but a lot can be implied in what is not said, and when emotions are running high, it's best to be aware of this sensitive dynamic. For every biological parent I've had the privilege of engaging with, the common denominator among them is shame.

Biological parents and foster parents may be coming from a different frame of reference, so it's important not to depend on subtle social cues to communicate together. Interacting with biological parents will give you increased opportunities to practice gently and directly saying what you mean. Yes, over time, actions do speak louder than words, but there is a time for words, especially when you first meet. It will help reassure bio-parents to hear you say, *"I'm not here to replace you. You're his mom. I'm here to take good care of him until you're able to do so."*

We are mindful to point out to our kids that just because someone isn't functioning at a safe and healthy level right now, it doesn't make them a "bad person," simply someone who is struggling. We are also intentional to point out that being unhealthy now doesn't mean a person will be in that place forever.

Remember that in building a relationship, you are still a mandatory reporter. If something that is shared with you isn't safe, you must pass it along to the appropriate people.

WHEN WHAT YOU OFFER ISN'T RECEIVED

While many biological parents soak up the small offerings of connection, it's very possible that a biological parent may not now, or ever be, in the place to honestly engage and take responsibility for what led to their child being in foster care. It's possible that the fear and hostility they feel towards themselves and towards the system will be directed at you, the foster parent, because you're the one who is with their child.

Show grace as much as possible. It's highly likely that they have noteworthy trauma and loss interwoven into their own history. A significant number of parents whose children have been removed from them have a personal history of being in foster care themselves. They may be genuinely fearful that their child will have their same experience in foster care, which may include being bounced around from home to home, moving schools often, not being treated respectfully, and not having their physical and emotional needs met.

WHERE OUR STORIES INTERSECT

Recognize that a biological parent will likely be named by their struggles and what led them to be Child Welfare involved before you ever meet them. *"This mom is homeless and addicted to drugs."* Realize that this doesn't solely define them, and recognize that the sharing doesn't go both ways. No caseworker will ever share with a biological parent, *"This foster parent caring for your child is a great person, but struggles with pride and is a workaholic."* Though the things we struggle with are not on the same level of unhealthy dysfunction that warrants Child Welfare involvement, I share this example to bring light to the truth that we all miss the mark in some way in life. Whether you know the details of a biological parent's history or not, compassionately remember that perhaps had you lived their same story and walked in their shoes, it could have been you in the same position they are in now. How would you hope that someone would interact with you?

HOW BACKGROUND INFLUENCES OUR LENS

Once you know the history of the parent, you may see behavior in their child that seems similar. Be careful not to view the child through the lens of their biological parent's shortcomings.

Unbeknownst to me, when one of my adopted children was in first grade, he stole a gift card from a chain store. Since it had not been paid for, it had no value. I learned of the incident when I heard him bragging to his neighborhood friends about his new "credit card." My internal, knee-jerk thought was, *"The apple doesn't fall far from the tree. He's going to go down the same road as his biological father and will be headed straight to jail one day."*

While it's easy to understand the connection of fear, I probably wouldn't have had that thought if his biological father's history was unknown. Also, my mind wouldn't have gone down this same path of fear had it been my biological child. Be aware of how you may be tempted to view your foster or adoptive child through the lens of their biological parent's shortcomings. After being triggered to envision the worst-case scenario for his future, I took a deep breath and replaced worry with the awe of my responsibility in teaching this child a new way. I called the store manager and told him that I was on my way back with a child who stole a gift card not worth anything, but we'd be returning it nonetheless. The manager had a caring, frank talk with my wide-eyed son about what would have happened had he been older and stolen something of true value. This was an opportune, teachable moment for my son. It also was one for me to see that my son is his own person and to reexamine my own lens of how knowing his biological parents' background influenced my first reaction.

CULTIVATING RELATIONSHIP SLOWLY

A foster parent may feel uncertainty such as, *"What if this biological parent finds out where I live and shows up at my door?"* This is a shadowy fear that turns out to be rare. In more than a decade and a half of fostering and having innumerable relationships with foster parents, I have heard rumblings of fear, but I don't know anyone for whom this has actually happened.

As you develop a relationship with a biological parent, ask for advice from the caseworker and others about the appropriateness of supervising visits or inviting a biological parent into your home. I encourage you to move slowly when it comes to inviting someone into the sacred space of your home. It's much easier to crack the door of relationship open incrementally, rather than swinging wide the door, only to later realize you want to shut it again. After you've exchanged eye contact, respectful hellos, and snippets of conversations, you can unhurriedly develop a relationship in small ways, such as exchanging email (you can set up a new account for this specific purpose), phone numbers and meeting in public places. Always get appropriate permission from your agency first.

Any caseworker who doesn't have safety concerns about the biological and foster parent meeting and is holistically-minded will see the benefit of relational bridge-building. There are plenty of caseworkers, however, who have never witnessed a foster parent and biological parent in collaboration. Even without any overt safety concerns, caseworkers may feel this is outside their comfort zone and perceive this as risky. If things go awry, it will be one more thing they have to deal with and because of this, they may prefer to keep parties separated.

Two summers ago, our family said yes to a sibling group of four ranging in age from 4-13. Our own four kids were in a similar age range. We knew this wasn't for the long haul, so we said yes to the chaos of having 8 kids for the week in order to buy the caseworker more time to keep them together and out of a hotel. We had an extra room with a bunk bed and two blow-up air mattresses.

On the day they were dropped off at my house, I asked the caseworker how the biological mom seemed to be coping. The caseworker told me she seemed calm and reasonable and didn't have any concerns about phone contact. I asked for the mom's phone number and said I would be happy to have the kids call her. I was careful not to have them call right before bed. In my experience, it's strategic to have kids talk with their parents during the daytime, where they can take in a conversation and then engage in other activities, rather than right before bedtime when emotions tend to run higher. All of the younger kids spoke with their mom, and then the teenager went up to the room we had prepared for her to talk privately, while the others bounced on the trampoline. After the kids finished talking, I took the phone, introduced myself, and said: *"Hi __, I'm Jillana. I imagine I'm talking to you on one of the worst days of your entire life, but I want you to know that while you're working on what you need to work on, and while the agency is working on a longer-term foster home solution, it's my honor to meet your beautiful kids. They were so polite when I first met them today. That makes me think that you've been a good mom and have just hit a rough patch right now..."* and that was all it took for the ice to be broken.

For the next week, as the kids called their mom regularly and filled her in on our activities, we spoke for a few minutes at the end of every call. When the agency found a longer-term home the following week, I was able to share with the new foster parent about the biological mom's receptiveness to talking with me. (If it were my kids, I'd absolutely be craving to know the name and hear the voice of the person caring for them; wouldn't you?) Subsequently, I've had the privilege of watching a caring connection develop between this biological mom and foster mom during the one year the kids were in foster care. The two moms' relational connection still flourishes now that the kids have returned home.

LOVE OFFERINGS

It's important to remember that most biological parents love their child, despite what brought them to the place of the state stepping in to ensure their child's basic care and safety. Even if a parent loses their parental rights by voluntarily relinquishing them or by court mandate, there are often real glimpses of love offered from within their capacity, which may look different than your capacity.

For one of my children, this love was offered from his birth mother, who brought a blanket from the Dollar Store to each of the three visits she had with him. She then disappeared, never to show up again. I will keep them forever. They are, however humble, a love offering to him.

SUPPORT

One of the beautiful aspects of developing a relationship over time with a biological parent is that the foster parent can be a source of support after a child is returned home. Parents who have their children taken into foster care, no matter the varying circumstances as to why, usually all have in common a level of isolation and a lack of true community in their life. Seeing foster parents continue to be a source of healthy community and respite gives much needed wrap-around support and encouragement to the biological parent. It also may assuage any sense of divided loyalty for the child to see both parents collaboratively engaging together. Despite all the many community service programs and classes parents need to engage before having their kids returned home, it's often the new coping skills learned *combined* with positive, healthy, *human connection* that gives the parent courage to break cycles and chart a new course.

In 2008, I met Jennifer at court as I was fostering her six-month-old son. I introduced myself to her and gave her an 8 x 10 photograph of her baby. She burst into tears and I found myself unexpectedly telling her that I was rooting for her. I surprised even myself in saying this. So began a relationship where I drove the baby to the Child Welfare office for supervised visits until Jennifer asked that I supervise visits outside the office. This was understandable given that she had grown up visiting her mom in the same DHS office and room where she was now visiting with her child. Over two years after our initial meeting and countless ups and downs, her rights were terminated. I held strong boundaries and there were seasons in which we were not in contact due to Jennifer's active drug use, but I was always glad to know her and have her know who was raising her son.

I later became a "relative" foster parent when the full biological brother of my adopted three-year-old was born. We fostered her next son, Elias, until he was court-ordered to be returned to her. We walked alongside her for four years, and then the same pattern of relapse emerged. We fostered and returned Elias twice, and against all odds, still remain in relationship.

There were some seasons that felt like a merry-go-round I wasn't sure I wanted to ride, and others where I was singing "The Hills are Alive" as in the opening number of *The Sound of Music.* There's so much to this story that I've written an entire book about it, but here's what I would say in summary: people often look at this head-turning, collaborative relationship I've had with Jennifer for more than decade and exclaim, "Wow! Look what you've done for *her!*" I can sincerely reply "Look what she's done for *me!*" I am not the same person I once was. My life has changed, and I am transformed through having her in my life.

You may have the desire to develop a relationship with a child's biological parent, but the biological parent may not be interested in this for a plethora of reasons. In foster care, there is much that is out of our control, and like all relationships, you have to keep the focus on what you can reasonably engage and try to let go of the rest.

Chapter Six

Foster Parenting & Interacting with Your Agency

AGENCY STAFF & THE "US VS. THEM" DYNAMIC

This particular strain of the "Us vs. Them" dynamic is extremely common. Unlike engaging with the biological parents, you will have no choice when it comes to interacting with your foster care agency.

Once you have opened your door and heart to a child, it may be tempting to think that the caseworker coming to check on this child once a month can't possibly "get" all the emotional complexities or needs of this child. After all, you are the one living with her 24/7. You know the child's knee-jerk reactions to things, her favorite color, her fears, what she reads before bed, and what she wants to do when she grows up. For caseworkers, despite how much their heart may be in it, your child will likely be one of dozens of children whose cases are sitting in a file on their desk. Due to this, caseworkers may have to double-check the name of the child before knocking on the foster parent's front door just to make sure they have it right. That felt dynamic of *"I know so much about this child and you only know the bare minimum"* can feel discouraging to foster parents and caseworkers alike.

There's a vast continuum in the way caseworkers and foster parents respond to one another that can set you up for either collaborative or combative engagement. I encourage you to remember the common humanity we all share. We can strive to interact in a way that alleviates one another's stress and thinks the best of one another, or we can be the ones to "dog pile" on each other's already burdened backs.

A common grievance among foster parents is being perceived as simply a glorified babysitter. Engaged, committed foster parents desire to feel like an integral part of the child's team.

COMMUNICATION & THE WORLD OF CHILD WELFARE

When you first meet your child's caseworker, I would encourage you to talk explicitly about the best way to communicate. Is it by phone or email? Will you text? It's a personal choice, but I always prefer email when communicating about important things with my child's caseworker because we then both have a written record of the correspondence and others can be copied in as needed. There are a lot of moving pieces and many professionals who need communication, so I'm all for the "one fell swoop" approach of getting on the same page versus individual phone calls.

It is entirely possible that within the first 24 hours of a child walking through your door, the child may reveal to you more than the caseworker is aware of, especially if this is the child's first time in foster care. Assume the best of the caseworker. It does not necessarily mean information was intentionally withheld. It is more likely that it wasn't shared because it wasn't known until the child shared it with you. You'll learn the importance of documenting important conversations in your foster parent training class.

Recently, a caseworker had to deliver hard news that she knew my friend, a fellow foster parent, would find devastating. She delivered it in person and then sat beside the foster parent on the couch in silence for a few minutes. Despite the inability to change the outcome, there was kindness. In this web of human interconnectedness, one of the most powerful experiences is to know that people are *with* us. Just as this caseworker showed this foster parent, we, in turn, as foster parents have endless opportunities to show this same compassion to those we rub shoulders with on this foster care journey.

The world of Child Welfare is often dark and bleak. Many enter this field with the high ideal of helping children in need. Some drawn to helping professions bring a personal drive to their work attempting to "right the wrongs" of their own childhood. No matter what initially drew someone to social work, it's usually just a matter of time before a caseworker's high ideals come crashing down to the low and harsh reality of small cubicles, fluorescent lighting, and the tyranny of the urgent work culture, with more paperwork stacked high on desks than can possibly be completed in any given day. Most people who chose "helping a child" as their profession didn't envision the tightrope reality so many in Child Welfare walk: checking boxes on paperwork, the pressures of court, trying to have some semblance of a personal relationship with the many children for whom they're the legal guardian, and a work culture chronically known for low morale.

It's very possible that along the way, you may encounter some professionals at Child Welfare who seem callous. Before I totally dismiss this as a choice, I will tell you that secondary trauma is real and so are its effects. A few of the many effects of secondary trauma can be apathy, hopelessness, and the inability to embrace complexity. While we as foster parents take on the particulars of one child's suffering, Child Welfare staff are privy to a fast-paced, relentless slew of heartbreaking details of children being abused, neglected, and abandoned daily. They are intimately acquainted with the underbelly of society and regularly see the faces of children, get to know their names, and hear their stories of the most egregious forms of neglect, and physical, emotional, and sexual abuse. Many see devastation first hand. They interview kids and repeatedly read and write reports containing hellacious details. Once they read, write and speak about these details they may never erase them from their memory. While foster parents experience children's horrific histories, perhaps at a deeper level, caseworkers daily confront an overwhelming barrage of brokenness.

The chances of someone devoting a significant portion of their life to work in Child Welfare and stepping away from the world of foster care unscathed by secondary trauma is next to nil. I offer this context to say that while people must be held to a reasonable standard to do their jobs, we need to have compassion, recognizing that this is a brutal field with high turnover rates due to burnout and secondary trauma.

Recognize that there's not a difference in pay for the ones who answer the phones with a tone that implies "I hate my life!" and respond with apathy versus those who serve you with warm, caring professionalism. I can honestly say that most of my foster care experience has been interacting with Child Welfare professionals who embody an intrinsic motivation to do good work with dogged determination to serve kids and families well, despite the heavy emotional toll of the work. I have also been on the receiving end of a caseworker who rarely returned any form of communication.

If you interact with someone going the extra mile for you or simply doing their job with excellence, despite a work atmosphere constrained by overwhelming demands, by all means, tell them! I strive to practice this often. It's always met with a genuine appreciation that someone has actually noticed.

BE KIND & ASSERTIVE

Embracing the mystery of foster care may take the form of quiet surrender, respectful advocacy, or kicking and screaming. It's highly likely that if you start driving down the road of foster care, you'll find yourself responding to this journey, which you can't fully control, in all of these ways at different points in your travels.

Despite whatever vibe you perceive from the caseworker who visits your home, I humbly offer you my personal mantra: "Be kind and assertive." Your voice is as an advocate for this child. There are times when your perspective may be warmly welcomed, and other times, it may be viewed as overstepping. Sometimes you'll be in agreement with the direction of the case plan (such as returning home to parent, adoption, or guardianship), but there may be other times that you cringe fearfully at the direction of the case plan. Please remember that sometimes caseworkers are in a bind, feel your same concern, but are bound by policy. It's all too easy for foster parents to demonize them, and likewise, for a caseworker not to think the best of a foster parent who may be stirring the waters by asking questions. By all means, advocate and make your voice heard on behalf of the child, including talking to appropriate higher-ups if you have concerns. Anything that needs to be voiced assertively, however, can still be communicated with a kind professionalism.

Over the years, I've seen the timeline of a case change repeatedly, which often tests foster parents' ability to be "kind and assertive" when interacting with the agency. A family may be asked to take a child for a certain amount of time, which rarely turns out to be exact.

The timeline you hear in regard to how long the children will stay with you is something you need to hold on to loosely. Nobody can look into a crystal ball and tell you with precise accuracy how long a child will be in your care. Most of the time, the timeline will be longer, not shorter, than originally thought. Depending on circumstances, this can cause difficulty for a multitude of reasons. We must remember that caseworkers don't have a crystal ball. They can make estimates, but so much of predicting a timeline is like a hypothetical chess game with unpredictable human factors. These factors can include when a bed will open up at a treatment facility or when an apartment will become available in a clean and sober housing complex. Caseworkers have little control over such circumstances when making their best guess about a time frame.

Another common reason a foster parent can lose their ability to be "kind and assertive" is because they've fallen in love with their foster child and want them to stay forever, which can put them at odds with the current case plan for the child.

In Oregon, the standard for which a biological parent needs to function in order to have a child returned is deemed "minimally adequate." This phrase can pulse fear through the veins of foster parents. For foster parents, they may be tempted to dwell on how this child will have their best shot at a stable life filled with opportunities, if they just remain with them forever.

I once heard a fired-up foster parent share, *"This child has her own room with a brand new bedspread and wooden letters of her name hanging up on this wall in our house. If she goes back home, she'll be in a 2 bedroom apartment with 8 people. How will this ever serve her well?"*

We have to remember that the core of foster care isn't about so-cio-economics. Foster care is not about who can offer that child more materially. If that were a justified concept, I'm pretty sure someone in a nearby gated community at the top of the hill has more to offer my kids than I do. The question at hand through-out the life of the court case is not, "Who can offer more to this child materially?" nor is it, "Where does the child have the brightest future?"

The main question at hand throughout the case will focus on whether the biological parents are doing their required services (such as parenting classes, addiction treatment, anger manage-ment, obtaining safe housing, etc.) in an adequate amount of time. Are the safety concerns that initially drew the child into foster care mitigated and will the parent be able to care for this child again at a minimally adequate standard? The custom letters hanging on the wall will never have anything to do with the case.

COURT & POLICY & BEST PRACTICE

In most cases, you are welcome to attend court, and I highly rec-ommend you do. The judge may ask you for an update on the child from your perspective. You can also request to be heard. Attending court allows you to hear and see things directly with-out having to rely solely on a caseworker to update you.

There is research that shows children have better long-term out-comes and feel more secure in their identity when placed with their biological families or relatives over foster parents with whom they have no blood-relation. The ever-present challenge you'll soon come to see is that right alongside the pull of your heart, there are multiple swirling complexities that come into play. These complicated intricacies include your state's elaborate Child Welfare policies, along with the court's timeline and over-sight in the life of a case. In addition, pitted against each other in many contentious Child Welfare decisions is this: a child's future in being placed with unknown blood relatives versus the child's healthy attachment to their current caregivers. As a foster parent, you may get a front-row seat to the core issues of identity and belonging, a child's current attachment, and public policy all tossed into a blender. If anyone claims this is easy-breezy stuff to talk about, they've never navigated this rugged terrain.

As a foster parent, if you have had the opportunity to build a relational bridge with the biological parent, your distress at the child returning home may be assuaged because of the likelihood that you'll continue to see the child. Nothing, however, is guaranteed after the child is returned, even if you try hard and give it the best shot. Ultimately, the ball is not in your court.

For many foster parents who have devoted a significant portion of their time and heart to a child, watching a child walk out of their door months or years later signaling a potential abrupt and forever goodbye is devastating. Heart-crushing entanglement can occur when you mix together fierce love, genuine concern, fear of the unknown, and anger at the inability to change the outcome. In the midst of sadness, and in an effort to try and encourage the foster parent, those in the foster parent's corner may try to offer well-meaning support by saying things like, *"Her mom doesn't even deserve her back!"*

It's easy to see how when you start interacting with these emotionally dicey dynamics, you're soon sitting squarely in the ditch of grief and feeling overwhelmed. As an American culture, we don't do grief well. Mix in all the misconceptions about foster care and the swirling emotional dynamics of this journey, and it can feel extra lonely.

Additionally, at times, there can feel like a great divide between the theory of "best practice" and the lived experience.

Our first foster placement was actually two brothers, the 12th and 15th children out of a sibling set of fifteen. We were glad to welcome the brothers together, and we had learned in our foster parent training class the importance of siblings being together. It was quickly very clear that the older sibling, age nine at the time, was heavily impacted by trauma which manifested in exasperating behaviors. He exited his bedroom window and ran away. The story of how terrified I felt while running the streets, calling his name, and talking with the police is a story for another time. After unsafe, violent episodes often targeted at his younger brother, the agency decided this particular child couldn't stay. I felt like a failure. Why didn't he want to stay? I knew cognitively it had very little to do with what he was being offered in our home and had everything to do with what he had taken in, lived, and borne witness to prior to ever walking in my front door. In this first placement with two brothers, I learned a painful lesson—that "best practice" doesn't always leave room for the lived reality.

Chapter Seven

We Gotta at Least Touch on This

GRIEF & LOSS

My friend, when you look at the words FOSTER CARE, don't miss the invisible print that starkly reads **GRIEF and LOSS** in bold, capital letters.

Despite changing variables, foster care always stems from the starting point of grief and loss. Something has already gone awry in a child's story in order for them to be in foster care. So, and I say this as gently as possible, don't be startled when grief and loss continue to be written into the narrative of your foster care journey.

For some, grief and loss may mean friends and family who do not understand or support your decision to foster and the changing of those relationships. It may mean staring in the chasm between how you dreamed family life would go and your current reality. It may be the loss of your independence. There is grief in wrestling through the fact that you must now daily engage in a completely different style of parenting than the one in which you were parented. It can feel hard and foreign, especially as others may judge. For some, grief follows an agonizing goodbye. For others, grief can mean a child stays and this parenting road is a lot rockier than anticipated—with steep hills blocking views of green pastures.

Let me be completely candid: signing up for foster care is an invitation to raise your hand and invite heartbreak and suffering into your life. Foster care gives you a front row seat to put on 3-D glasses to an appalling reality of abuse and neglect. It allows you to see what is happening underneath the surface in your very own community. Even with being intentional, creating margins, discerning well, preparing yourself for comments, and striving to be collaborative, let me say this with gentle boldness: you will not be inoculated from heavy-heartedness on your fostering journey. In the moments or seasons of anguish that will assuredly come, you'll have to free-fall back into your initial "why."

A QUICK WORD ABOUT ADOPTION

If you believe you would be emotionally broken beyond repair if you had to welcome in, love, and then say goodbye to a child, there's no shame in that. I would encourage you not to foster, but to instead consider adoption.

The goal of foster care is to return a child to their biological family. Foster parents *may* have the ability to become the adoptive parents of their child in foster care, but it bears repeating – the very goal of foster care is to return a child to their biological family. If you're getting into foster care with your heart's deepest desire that a child will stay with you forever, I would encourage you to go straight to the adoption route. Engaging in foster care with the hope of adoption may make it challenging for you to engage with the biological parents in a healthy way. I feel protective of your extra high potential for heartbreak. There are plenty of deserving kids for whom you may be just the right adoptive fit.

THE MYTH OF THE CLEAN SLATE

Especially prevalent in the adoption and foster care community is the ill, preconceived notion of a clean slate, especially with younger kids. While we know about the indelible imprint of trauma on the brain and body, it can be tempting for foster, and especially adoptive parents, to buy into the myth that there's a formula. This formula is that the perfect amount of faith, love, nurture, and structure will suddenly overcome and wipe clean a child's slate, erasing their traumatic past. Regrettably, there isn't ever a perfect formula to overthrow the past, no matter how much goodness and intentionality is poured into the mix. This doesn't mean that we don't do all we can to learn about their histories and parent them in trauma-informed ways to help them attempt to overcome their background. Yet, as parents, we need to be mindful of the gap between our subtle expectation that with time and consistency, the history of what brought them into foster care will fade like chalk on a blackboard.

How will it affect *you* if despite your best loving efforts, the effects of trauma remain prominently inscribed on a child's slate? Consciously or not, the roots of loss sprout up within all foster care and adoption stories. Be aware of how you may be buying into the clean-slate myth.

MY OWN PUBLIC SERVICE ANNOUNCEMENT

Become educated about in-utero alcohol exposure. It is not surprising to learn that major harm can be done through a woman abusing drugs while pregnant. Many are surprised to hear, however, that drinking during pregnancy can cause lifelong, irreparable brain damage. Many caseworkers will document that a woman abused illegal substances while pregnant, yet never specifically ask her about the cheap, legal substance known to cause the most damage in-utero. If a person is known to be abusing illegal substances while pregnant, chances are high that she is also abusing something cheap and legal that is easy to find. The specific effects of alcohol exposure in-utero are daunting and immense.

In case worker and foster parent training alike, "drugs and alcohol" are often lumped together in a short, insufficient training session. Most caseworkers and foster parents know very little about this brain-based disability, despite a higher prevalence of kids suffering from in-utero exposure issues in the foster and adoptive community. It is tricky that the main symptoms of alcohol exposure are behaviorally-based, not physical signs, as less than 5% of kids affected by in-utero alcohol abuse have physical markers. Since kids entering foster care understandably have behaviors due to the trauma they endured, foster parents and caseworkers alike may be tempted to think the impulsivity, aggression, inability to make cause-and-effect connections, and many behavioral concerns will improve with time. **While there may be some progress made due to a stable home environment, there is no undoing brain damage.** (*Please re-read that last sentence!*) As parents, it's critical that we have the right, compassionate lens to see our kids so we can use the right strategies to parent them. The very lens through which we see children affects the way we interact with them.

Kids who have suffered in-utero alcohol abuse are at higher risk of being abused themselves due to their exasperating behaviors. They also run a higher risk of disrupted adoptions. Go with your gut if you feel that, in addition to trauma, there is more going on than meets the eye. Educate yourself about the vast symptoms of in-utero alcohol exposure and advocate relentlessly for the support you and your child need.

REST

When a child leaves your home, you may decide to "take a break." If you discern this is what you need, by all means do it. Nobody else will have a pulse on this better than you. Chances are high that immediately after a child walks out your door, you may get a call for another child in need, or more realistically, you'll receive that call while that other child is still there. This is where having a good, collaborative relationship with your agency is key. Despite the desperate need, if your foster care agency has a protective eye on your sustainability, they will respect you by not buzzing your cell phone when you've asked for a breather.

Protect yourself from burnout by not shying away from rest, thinking you can engage foster care like the energizer bunny and override your body's natural need for recuperation. Despite a good heart, strong voice, loving presence, and assertive advocacy, there will always be a need to pace yourself. Nobody else can do that for you. Don't let others' comments about bravery tie an imaginary superhero cape around your neck to try and fool you otherwise. Take time to refuel.

WHAT IF MY FOSTER CARE JOURNEY ISN'T A "SUCCESS STORY?"

We all love a perfect Hollywood script where there's an insurmountable struggle, the protagonist overcomes, the lights fade, music starts, and the credits roll.

But what happens if you feel like you are giving your all in coming alongside vulnerable children—and potentially their parents—and there's no evidence of making a difference?

For this, I will quote what my wise husband, Luke, wrote years ago in a personal paper he entitled *Guiding Principles for a Theology of Foster Care:*

If we approach foster care like our culture teaches us to approach other aspects of our lives—work, family, education—in which we create our own success, we are doomed to burnout and failure. Children who have experienced the trauma of abuse or neglect, or have been exposed to alcohol or drugs in utero, may never live up to our conditioned understanding of 'success.' Similarly, their birth parents, who in many cases have established lifelong habits of unhealthy behaviors, may never 'get their act together' in the ways we might hope. If we approach the milieu of foster care with only a results-oriented mindset, we will experience nothing but frustration.

Instead, recognizing that 'where there is love, God breaks in' allows us to do all we can to pursue wholeness and health spiritually, emotionally, physically, and socially in the lives of children and families out of love—without it being measured by results, change, or success. Viewing our interaction with children and families through the lens of relationship, instead of rescue, allows us to weather the ups and downs of growth, change, and failure while not being discouraged from our divine calling to love.

Some of my dear friends were able to recognize recently the humanity of their child's birth parents, even though they met them shackled in court, relinquishing their parental rights. My friends requested twenty minutes together with the biological parents, where they could record what they wanted their son to know about them. They asked the biological parents about their favorite foods, music preferences and things they were most proud of (which included the father's once-in-a-lifetime opportunity to airbrush a moose skull). As the corrections officer gave them a two-minute warning before time was up, the biological parents said quietly, *"As you raise our son, we hope you'll tell him that we loved him...and that we weren't always like this...thank you for asking for the time to get to know us. And we're glad he's with you.*" Then for the sake of the child, they all took several photos, even some selfies—both serious and silly—for the foster (forthcoming adoptive) parents to show to their son one day. This took my breath away when I saw the photos with their tattooed faces, leaning in close together, not only because of the heart-wrenching exchange of raw humanity, but because the biological parents were known white supremacists with "PRIDE" inked all over their bodies. My friend is a person of color.

Because of the divine imprint on all people, no matter how buried it may seem, the experiences and stories of every human being possess something to reveal and teach us.

WE MAY NEVER KNOW OUR INFLUENCE

My husband and I started fostering in New York in 2003. The first child I ever had the privilege of parenting came to me at age six—a toothless first grader, the youngest of 15 biological siblings. Other than the one year he lived with us, he spent his entire childhood away from us. Now we are back in one another's lives as reclaimed family.

I hear the memories from his perspective of our short time living together. It doesn't surprise me to hear of the big events such as going to Disneyland or the bike he received for Christmas. Most surprising to me is his remembrance of the small things like grilled cheese sandwiches eaten around the table, the Spiderman poster hung in the bedroom, the scooter ridden in the driveway, the brownies baked in the kitchen.

There's so much to this still unfolding journey of re-defining family, I've written a book that shares more of it. For now, however, I want you to know this: **Though it's easy to think otherwise, it's possible that what is being planted in being a foster family is**

deeper than simply being under the same roof for a season.

THE PRIVILEGE OF BEING A TENSION-HOLDER

Your invitation on this foster care journey is to become an eyes-wide-open Tension-Holder.

You'll be invited to hold inevitable tension as you navigate relationships and create space to be intentional with yourself, your own family, the child, the biological parent, and those with whom you're interacting at your foster care agency.

The human compulsion to want to "fit in" is a real one, and at the core of foster care is an invitation for your life to look different. Be aware that there may be times when gazing in the rear view mirror at the smoother road you left behind may unknowingly invite bitterness to travel with you.

If you are intentional to stave off anger and bitterness, being engaged in foster care will allow you to see and experience the simultaneous ache and beauty of this world, the constant tug of the *now* and the hope for the *not yet.*

As you endeavor to travel this journey with open palms and eyes searching for redemption, wholeness, and healing in the midst of the suffering, foster care will invite you to be keenly attuned to divine grace. Know that rarely does hope sit in front of you like a boulder in the middle of the road. Sometimes hope may take the form of a pebble. You may have to squint to see it, but it is nonetheless present on the path.

If you receive glimpses of hope, strive to pass that discovery along to others. We all need it. Emily Dickinson tells us, "Hope is the thing with feathers that perches in the soul." You can engage the pain and somber reality of foster care, and still be filled with tenacious hope.

In clinging to hope and to your "why," you may even learn to live in this sacred place of surrender with a striking calm—holding onto the mess, your faith, and your reality.

Anne Lamott writes: "This is the most profound spiritual truth I know: that even when we're sure that love can't conquer all, it seems to anyway. It goes down into the rat hole with us, in the guise of our friends, and there it swells and comforts. It gives us second winds, third winds, hundredth winds."[2]

The ebb and flow of this foster care journey through sixteen years of names, stories, and snippets of exchanged humanity between children, biological parents, caseworkers, and the dynamics of my own family have been my constant perspective-giver. It's humbled me to be slower to judge and quicker to exude more compassion, seeing complexities from multiple sides. It's fired me up to mentor other foster parents and be a part of invoking change in the way the community and Child Welfare engage with one another on a state-wide scale.

So, in conclusion, I return to my original fifteen-second dialogue with Ms. Coffee-with-a-splash-of-cream asking me about foster care before dashing off. How I answered was true, and yet the inadequacy of our fleeting dialogue lingered.

Has it been hard?

Yes.

Has it been worth it?

"It's difficult, AND it's worth it."

While this is hardly a comprehensive summary of all I have learned, I hope this letter has helped to round out the inadequacy

---

2 Lamott, Anne. Traveling Mercies: Some Thoughts on Faith. Anchor Books, 2006, p.64.

of that fleeting dialogue. Everything I've shared with you is what I wish I'd been told before signing up to become a foster parent in 2003. After more than a decade-and-a-half of living this journey, I hope this insight will give you pause and help you discern next steps, no matter where you are on your foster care journey.

Foster care is a constant invitation to walk a precarious tight-rope between reality and hope.

Blessings to you, my friend, as you engage and discern what is yours to do in the midst of the privilege and the heartbreak on this challenging and worthy parenting road less-traveled.

— Jillana

READ THE STORIES THAT LED TO THIS INSIGHT.

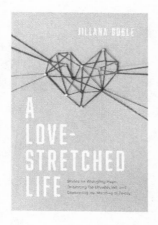

With honesty, faith, and a dose of humor, the compilation of stories in Jillana's debut memoir, *A Love-Stretched Life,* will stay with you as you strive to love and to love well, even when—and especially when—it's hard. Whether you are widening your family circle or just trying to get through the day, Jillana welcomes you to her table, offering you an anchor of hope to hang on to as you navigate your own love-stretched life.

Acknowledgments

In the midst of writing *A Love-Stretched Life* which shares my personal narrative of how foster care, adoption, trauma and special needs have indelibly shaped my life, I realized I also needed to write *No Sugar-Coating: The Coffee Talk You Need About Foster Parenting.* Through recalling my own story and from innumerable conversations with prospective and current foster parents, I saw a need to compile in one place snippets of practical tips, hard-fought wisdom, and insight I've learned along the way.

I am grateful to the many who cheered me on in the writing of this little book. I've carried your encouragement with me with in the early mornings and late nights spent at the computer as I decided to do a little writing "on the side" in the midst of an already incredibly full life!

My sincere gratitude to colleagues and fellow foster parent friends who graciously agreed to be manuscript readers and give valuable feedback. Thanks to Miriam, Frannie, Anani, Louise, Lacey, Seth, Anne, Kat, Sara, Emily and Nick.

To the many engaged with Embrace Oregon & Every Child, it's an honor to be in this space with you. Getting a front row seat to the many ways you show up is a privilege.

To my friends who know the real deal scoop behind the stories—you know who you are—you help give me, in Anne Lamott's words, my "hundredth winds." You make this life journey lighter and sweeter with our collective sharing of life's ups and downs.

Jennifer, who would have thought we'd be where we are today since meeting at court 11 years ago? Through all the mountains and valleys, we've learned and grown. I love you and I'm grateful for you.

To my children who have shaped and stretched me and given me so much joy, it's my greatest privilege to be your mom! I love and adore you! Thank you for continuing to teach me about what matters most in life.

And to Luke, who has been steadfast with love and support on this crazy adventure. Truthfully, we never may have started down this fostering road if we had gotten future glimpses into what some of our days would hold. Our lives would have been simpler, no doubt, but we also would have missed out on so much we now hold dear.

About the Author

Jillana Goble has been a foster mom, biological mom, and adoptive mom—in that order—since 2003. She is a connector and a collaborator who has walked an unlikely path in creating an unprecedented relationship with the children who have walked through her front door, their biological families, and with the Oregon Department of Human Services Child Welfare. She founded Embrace Oregon, which is the catalyst for Every Child Oregon, a robust engagement model bridging the community and foster care.

Jillana is the author of *A Love-Stretched Life: Wrangling Hope, Embracing the Unexpected, and Discovering the Meaning of Family.* She holds a Masters Degree in Teaching and is a sought after speaker on various topics around foster care, government & community partnership, adoption, special needs, grief, and hope. She continues to mentor and walk alongside countless foster parents navigating this journey.

Jillana and her husband, Luke, got married in 2000. They have two biological daughters and two sons that they fostered and later adopted. They were also reunited with their first son in foster care after over a decade apart. They are joyfully called "Auntie" & "Papa" by another child in foster care who has lived with them twice.

When not engaging with her family, Jillana enjoys drinking coffee with friends—half filled with cream—at neighborhood coffee shops. Her favorite things include leaning in to engage others' real deal stories, walking her sweet yet stubborn labradoodle around her city block, and reading in the tub way too late at night.

Connect with Jillana

WEB: JILLANA-GOBLE.COM
FB: JILLANA GOBLE – AUTHOR
IG: @JILLANAGOBLE

Made in the USA
Columbia, SC
14 May 2022